FAST CAKES

KÖNEMANN

One-bowl cakes

Mix up these speedy cakes made in one bowl, following the directions in the recipes, and you'll effortlessly produce the lightest sponges, hearty fruit cakes, muffins or moist sour cream or chocolate cakes.

Victoria Sponge

Preparation time:
  8 minutes
Total cooking time:
  20 minutes
*Makes one 20 cm
round sandwich cake*

125 g unsalted butter,
  chopped
1/2 cup caster sugar
3 eggs, lightly beaten
1 cup self-raising flour
*1 teaspoon baking
  powder*
1/2 cup strawberry jam
icing sugar

1 Preheat oven to moderate 180°C. Brush two shallow 20 cm round sandwich tins with melted butter or oil. Line base with paper; grease paper.
2 Using electric beaters, beat unsalted butter and sugar in a small mixing bowl until light and creamy. Add eggs gradually, beating thoroughly after each addition.
3 Add the sifted dry ingredients to bowl. Beat on low speed for 30 seconds, then high speed 1 minute or until the mixture is thick and creamy.
4 Pour mixture evenly into prepared tins; smooth surface. Bake 20 minutes or until sponge is lightly golden and shrinks from side of tin. Turn onto wire rack to cool.
5 Spread top of one cake layer with jam; top with remaining layer. Dust lightly with icing sugar before serving.

Note: For a lighter sponge, sift flour three times before combining with the remaining ingredients. Sponge cakes are best eaten the day they are made. Keep in a cool, dry place until ready to serve.

*Victoria Sponge (top) and
Fruit Medley Loaf (see page 4).*

Fruit Medley Loaf

Preparation time:
  8 minutes + 5 minutes
  standing
Total cooking time:
  40 minutes
Makes one
25 x 15 cm loaf

1¼ *cups (200 g) All*
  Bran cereal
⅔ *cup hot milk*
½ *cup finely chopped*
  dried apples
1 *cup mixed dried fruit*
¼ *cup pumpkin kernels*
  (pepitas)
⅔ *cup soft brown sugar*
3 *eggs, lightly beaten*
1 *teaspoon ground*
  mixed spice
½ *cup wholemeal self-*
  raising flour

1 Preheat oven to
moderately hot 210°C/
190°C gas. Brush a
25 x 15 x 5.5 cm loaf
tin with melted butter
or oil. Line the base
and sides with paper;
grease paper.
2 Place bran and milk
in a large mixing bowl,
stir with a wooden
spoon. Leave, uncovered,
for 5 minutes or until
almost all the milk has
been absorbed.
3 Add fruit, kernels,
sugar, eggs, spice and
flour to bran mixture.
Beat with a wooden
spoon 3 minutes or
until ingredients are
well combined.

4 Spoon mixture into
prepared tin. Bake for
40 minutes or until a
skewer comes out clean
when inserted in centre
of cake. Turn cake onto
wire rack to cool. Serve
sliced with butter.

Note: This loaf can be
stored for up to three
days in an airtight
container.

Carrot and Pecan Cake

Preparation time:
  15 minutes
Total cooking time:
  45 minutes
Makes one 20 cm
square cake

2 *eggs, lightly beaten*
2 *cups grated carrot*
2 *teaspoons grated*
  orange rind
⅔ *cup chopped pecan*
  nuts
½ *teaspoon ground*
  cinnamon
⅓ *cup orange juice*
½ *cup oil*
⅔ *cup caster sugar*
1⅓ *cups self-raising*
  flour

1 Preheat oven to
moderate 180°C. Brush
a shallow, 20 cm square
cake tin with melted
butter or oil, line base
with paper; grease
paper.
2 Place eggs, carrot,
rind, nuts, cinnamon,

juice, oil and sugar in
large mixing bowl.
Using a wooden spoon,
stir to combine.
3 Sift flour into bowl.
Beat with wooden
spoon 1 minute or until
mixture is thick and
ingredients are well
combined.
4 Spoon the mixture
evenly into prepared
tin; smooth surface.
Bake 45 minutes or
until skewer comes out
clean when inserted in
centre of cake. Turn
onto wire rack to cool.
Serve warm or cold.

Note: Decorate with
Cream Cheese Icing (see
page 63) and chopped
pecans, if liked.

Choc-centre Muffins

Preparation time:
  10 minutes
Total cooking time:
  15 minutes
Makes 15 muffins

2 *cups self-raising flour*
½ *cup caster sugar*
120 *g grated milk*
  chocolate
2 *eggs*
2 *teaspoons vanilla*
  essence
80 *g unsalted butter,*
  melted
1 *cup sour cream*
100 *g dark chocolate,*
  cut in squares
2 *tablespoons choc bits*

Carrot and Pecan Cake (top) and Choc-centre Muffins.

1 Preheat oven to moderate 180°C. Brush melted butter or oil into fifteen 1/2-cup capacity muffin cups.
2 Place flour, sugar, chocolate, eggs, essence, butter and sour cream in small mixing bowl. Using electric beaters, beat 1 minute on low speed or until just combined. Beat on high speed 1 minute.
3 Spoon half the mixture into prepared muffin cups. Place a piece of chocolate in the centre of each; top with remaining mixture.

4 Press choc bits onto top of each muffin. Bake 15 minutes or until puffed and lightly browned. Serve warm for a melted chocolate centre, or cool on a wire rack. These muffins are best served on the day of baking.

Lemon Butter Sandwich

Preparation time:
  10 minutes
Total cooking time:
  25 minutes
*Makes one 20 cm
round cake*

3 eggs
1/2 cup caster sugar
1/2 teaspoon lemon
  essence
1 cup self-raising flour
30 g unsalted butter,
  melted
1/2 cup cream cheese,
  softened
1/3 cup prepared lemon
  butter
icing sugar

1 Preheat oven to moderate 180°C. Brush a deep 20 cm round cake tin with melted butter or oil, line base with paper; grease paper.
2 Using electric beaters, beat the eggs, sugar and lemon essence in a small mixing bowl on high speed 5 minutes or until mixture is pale, thick and glossy. Using a metal spoon, gently fold in flour then butter. Mix lightly and quickly until smooth.
3 Spread mixture into prepared tin. Bake for 25 minutes or until sponge is lightly golden and shrinks from side of tin. Turn onto a wire rack to cool.

4 When cool, cut cake crossways into two even layers using a serrated knife. Spread one layer with cream cheese, then with lemon butter. Cover with remaining cake layer. Sprinkle with icing sugar to serve.

Date and Walnut Squares

Preparation time:
  10 minutes
Total cooking time:
  35 minutes +
  5 minutes standing
Serves 6

1 cup (130 g) finely
  chopped walnuts
1 cup (150 g) finely
  chopped dried
  dates
1/3 cup soft brown
  sugar
2 eggs, lightly beaten
1/3 cup oil
1/2 cup plain yoghurt
1 1/2 cups self-raising
  flour
1 tablespoon caster
  sugar
1/2 teaspoon ground
  cinnamon

1 Preheat oven to moderate 180°C. Brush a shallow 27 x 18 cm cake tin with melted butter or oil. Cover base with paper, extending over two sides; grease paper.
2 Place all but a quarter cup of walnuts in large mixing bowl with the dates and sugar. Add eggs, oil, yoghurt and sifted flour. Using a wooden spoon, beat 2 minutes or until the ingredients are well combined and the mixture is almost smooth.
3 Spoon mixture into prepared tin; smooth surface. Combine caster sugar and cinnamon. Sprinkle cinnamon sugar and reserved walnuts over the surface of the cake.
4 Bake 35 minutes or until a skewer comes out clean when inserted in centre of cake. Leave cake in tin 5 minutes before lifting onto wire rack to cool. When cool cut into squares.

Note: Date and Walnut Squares can be stored for up to two days in an airtight container. Serve cake with a dollop of whipped cream sweetened with a little caster sugar and vanilla, if liked.

---

*Lemon Butter Sandwich (top) and
Date and Walnut Squares.*

Strawberry and Cream Muffins

Preparation time:
  15 minutes
Total cooking time:
  30 minutes +
  5 minutes standing
Makes 8 muffins

2 eggs
¹/4 cup oil
2 tablespoons
  strawberry jam
¹/4 cup strawberry
  yoghurt
¹/2 cup caster sugar
1³/4 cups self-raising
  flour
100 g cream cheese
¹/4 cup strawberry jam,
  extra
strawberries, to
  decorate

1 Preheat oven to moderate 180°C. Brush melted butter or oil into eight ²/3-cup capacity muffin cups.

2 Place eggs, oil, jam, yoghurt and sugar in a large mixing bowl. Using a wooden spoon, beat mixture 1 minute or until well combined. Add sifted flour, stir until just combined; do not overbeat.

3 Place 2–3 tablespoons of mixture into each muffin cup. Cut cheese into eight pieces. Place a piece in the centre of each muffin. Top each piece with 2 teaspoons jam. Divide remaining mixture evenly between muffins. Bake for 30 minutes or until muffins are puffed and lightly golden. Stand 5 minutes in tin before turning onto wire rack to cool. To serve, dust muffins with sifted icing sugar; decorate with strawberries.

Note: Top muffins with Cream Cheese Icing (see page 63), if liked.

Strawberry and Cream Muffins.

Combine eggs, oil, jam, yoghurt and sugar in a large mixing bowl.

Divide batter between muffin cups and place a piece of cream cheese in each.

Top each piece of cheese with strawberry jam and cover with remaining mixture.

Decorate finished muffins with sifted icing sugar.

Banana Apple Muffins

Preparation time:
  12 minutes
Total cooking time:
  25 minutes
Makes 12 muffins

1/2 cup plain wholemeal
  flour
2/3 cup wholemeal self-
  raising flour
2/3 cup caster sugar
1/4 teaspoon ground
  nutmeg
1 large ripe banana,
  mashed
1/2 cup coarsely grated
  green apple
2 eggs, lightly beaten
1/2 cup oil
3/4 cup buttermilk

1 Preheat oven to moderate 180°C. Brush melted butter or oil into twelve 1/3-cup capacity muffin cups.
2 Place flours, sugar and nutmeg into a large mixing bowl. Make a well in centre; add fruit. Combine eggs, oil and buttermilk in a bowl or jug. Pour all at once into dry ingredients. Using a wooden spoon, stir for 1 minute or until ingredients are just combined; do not overbeat.
3 Spoon mixture into prepared muffin tins, filling two-thirds full. Bake for 25 minutes or until puffed and lightly golden. Turn onto wire rack to cool.

Note: Muffins can be decorated with Cream Cheese Icing (see page 63) and topped with banana chips, if liked.

Chocolate Fleck Butter Cake

Preparation time:
  20 minutes
Total cooking time:
  45 minutes
Makes one 23 cm round cake

150 g unsalted butter
2/3 cup caster sugar
1 tablespoon brandy
3 eggs, lightly beaten
1 teaspoon baking
  powder
2 1/4 cups self-raising
  flour
125 g milk chocolate,
  coarsely grated
1/3 cup milk
2/3 cup cream

1 Preheat oven to moderate 180°C. Brush a deep 23 cm round cake tin with melted butter or oil, line base with paper; grease paper.
2 Using electric beaters, beat butter, sugar and brandy in mixing bowl until light and creamy. Add the eggs gradually, beating thoroughly after each addition. Add sifted dry ingredients, chocolate and milk all at once. Beat on low speed for 1 minute or until just combined.
3 Spoon mixture into prepared tin; smooth surface. Bake for 45 minutes or until a skewer comes out clean when inserted in centre of cake. Turn onto wire rack to cool. When cool, cut the cake into three even layers using a serrated knife.
4 Using electric beaters, beat cream in small bowl until firm peaks form. Place first cake layer on a board. Spread cake evenly with half the cream, repeat with second cake layer and remaining cream and top with third cake layer. Decorate if liked and serve immediately.

Note: To decorate, ice cake with Chocolate Glacé Icing (see page 62) or Rich Chocolate Icing (see page 63). Top icing with roughly chopped nuts, if desired.

Chocolate Fleck Butter Cake (top) and Banana Apple Muffins.

Sultana Cakes

Preparation time:
 5 minutes
Total cooking time:
 12 minutes
Makes 18

1 1/3 cups self-raising
 flour
1/3 cup caster sugar
2/3 cup sultanas
1 egg, lightly beaten
1/4 cup cream
40 g unsalted butter,
 melted
1 teaspoon vanilla
 essence

1 Preheat oven to
moderate 180°C.
Lay out 18 paper patty
cases on deep patty tins
or oven trays.
2 Sift flour into large
mixing bowl, add sugar
and sultanas. Make a
well in the centre. Pour
combined egg, cream,
butter and essence into
bowl all at once.
Using a wooden spoon,
beat for 2 minutes or
until all the ingredients
are well combined; do
not overbeat.
3 Place a tablespoonful
of mixture into each
patty case. Bake for
12 minutes or until a
skewer comes out clean
when inserted in centre
of cakes. Turn onto
wire rack to cool. Serve
warm or cold.

Citrus Yoghurt Cake

Preparation time:
 10 minutes
Total cooking time:
 40 minutes
*Makes one 23 cm
ring cake*

150 g unsalted butter
2 teaspoons grated
 orange rind
1 teaspoon grated
 lemon rind
3/4 cup caster sugar
2 eggs, lightly beaten
1/3 cup ground almonds
1 2/3 cups self-raising
 flour, sifted
3/4 cup plain yoghurt

1 Preheat oven to
moderate 180°C.
Brush a 23 cm baba
tin with melted butter
or oil.
2 Using electric beaters,
beat butter, rinds and
sugar in small bowl
until light and creamy.
Add eggs gradually,
beating thoroughly
after each addition.
Add almonds, flour and
yoghurt all at once.
Beat for 1 minute on
low speed or until well
combined.
3 Spoon into prepared
tin. Bake 40 minutes or
until skewer comes out
clean when inserted in
centre of cake. Turn
onto wire rack to cool.

Citrus Yoghurt Cake (top) and Sultana Cakes.

Passionfruit Sour Cream Cake

Preparation time:
  10 minutes
Total cooking time:
  45 minutes
*Makes one 20 cm
round cake*

100 g unsalted butter
1/3 cup caster sugar
2 eggs, lightly beaten
2/3 cup passionfruit pulp
  in syrup
1 teaspoon grated
  lemon rind
1/2 cup sour cream
1 3/4 cups self-raising
  flour

1 Preheat oven to
moderate 180°C. Brush
a deep 20 cm round
cake tin with melted
butter or oil, line base
with paper; grease paper.
2 Using electric beaters,
beat butter and sugar in
small mixing bowl until
light and creamy. Add
eggs gradually, beating
thoroughly after each
addition. Add the
undrained pulp and
grated rind; beat until
just combined.
3 Add sour cream and
flour. Beat on low speed
30 seconds or until the
ingredients are just
combined. Beat on high
speed 1 minute or until
mixture is smooth. Do
not overbeat.
4 Spoon mixture into
prepared tin; smooth

surface. Bake for
45 minutes or until
skewer comes out clean
when inserted in centre
of cake. Turn cake onto
wire rack to cool.

Note: To decorate, top
with Passionfruit Glacé
Icing or Cream Cheese
Icing (see pages 62 and
63) or serve with a
dollop of whipped
cream mixed with a
little passionfruit pulp.

Almond Cherry Loaf

Preparation time:
  10 minutes
Total cooking time:
  40 minutes +
  5 minutes standing
*Makes one 23 x 13 cm
loaf*

90 g cream cheese,
  softened
30 g unsalted butter
1/2 cup caster sugar
1 egg
1 teaspoon almond
  essence
2/3 cup quartered glacé
  cherries
2/3 cup flaked almonds
1 cup self-raising flour
2 tablespoons milk

1 Preheat oven to
moderately hot 210°C/
190°C gas. Brush a
23 x 13 x 7 cm loaf tin
with melted butter or
oil. Cover base with
paper, extending over
two sides; grease paper.
2 Using electric beaters,
beat cheese, butter,
sugar, egg and essence
in small mixing bowl
for 5 minutes or until
light and creamy.
3 Add cherries, flaked
almonds, flour and
milk to bowl all at
once. Using a wooden
spoon, stir until
ingredients are well
combined and mixture
is almost smooth.
4 Spoon mixture into
the prepared tin;
smooth surface. Bake
for 40 minutes or until
skewer comes out clean
when inserted in centre
of cake. Leave cake in
tin 5 minutes before
turning onto wire rack
to cool. Decorate as
desired.

Note: To make this
cake using a wooden
spoon, beat cream
cheese, butter and sugar
in small mixing bowl
10 minutes or until
light and creamy. Add
egg and almond essence,
beat well. Add all the
remaining ingredients,
stir until well mixed
and bake as directed.

*Almond Cherry Loaf (top) and
Passionfruit Sour Cream Cake.*

Basic Chocolate Cake

Preparation time:
  12 minutes
Total cooking time:
  55 minutes
Makes one 20 cm
round cake

125 g unsalted butter
1 cup caster sugar
1 egg
2 teaspoons vanilla
  essence
1/3 cup cocoa powder
1 teaspoon baking
  powder
1 1/2 cups self-raising
  flour
3/4 cup cream

1 Preheat oven to moderate 180°C. Brush a deep 20 cm round cake tin with melted butter or oil, line base with paper; grease the paper.
2 Using electric beaters, beat butter and sugar in small mixing bowl until light and creamy. Add egg and vanilla essence; beat for 1 minute on medium speed or until well combined.
3 Add the sifted dry ingredients and cream to bowl. Beat on low speed for 1 minute or until just combined. Beat 2 minutes on high speed until smooth.

4 Spoon mixture into prepared tin; smooth surface. Bake for 55 minutes or until skewer comes out clean when inserted in centre of cake. Turn onto wire rack to cool.

Note: Ice with Chocolate Glacé Icing (see page 62) and decorate, if desired, with flaked chocolate and a dusting of icing sugar.

Apple and Fruit Cake

Preparation time:
  10 minutes
Total cooking time:
  1 hour
Makes one 20 cm
round cake

2 medium cooking
  apples
1 cup sugar
1 cup sultanas or mixed
  fruit
1 teaspoon cinnamon
  or mixed spice
1 1/2 cups self-raising
  flour
2 eggs, beaten
60 g butter, melted and
  cooled

1 Preheat oven to moderate 180°C. Brush 20 cm round cake tin with melted butter.
2 Peel and core apples and slice thinly. Place apples in large mixing bowl with sugar, sultanas, cinnamon, flour, beaten eggs and butter. Mix well with a wooden spoon.
3 Spoon mixture into prepared tin. Bake for 1 hour or until a skewer comes out clean when inserted in centre of the cake. Turn out to cool on wire rack.

Note: Ice with Lemon Cream Cheese Icing (see page 63). For a fancier finish, cut rind of one lemon into thin strips and arrange on top of the cake.

> ### HINT
> When storing a freshly cooked cake, let it reach room temperature before placing it in an airtight container. The cake should fit snugly into the container, to minimise the air space around it and keep it fresh longer, and should be stored in a cool, dry place. Cakes should not be kept in the refrigerator unless specified in the recipe.

Apple and Fruit Cake (top)
and Basic Chocolate Cake.

Golden Syrup and Hazelnut Cake

Preparation time:
  12 minutes
Total cooking time:
  35 minutes +
  5 minutes standing
Makes one 20 cm square cake

3/4 cup chopped
  hazelnuts
60 g unsalted butter
1/3 cup golden syrup
125 g unsalted butter,
  extra
1/3 cup golden syrup,
  extra
1 egg
1/4 cup ground hazelnuts
1 2/3 cups self-raising
  flour
1/3 cup milk

1 Preheat oven to moderate 180°C. Brush a shallow 20 cm square cake tin with melted butter or oil, line base with paper; grease paper.
2 Scatter the chopped hazelnuts over base of prepared tin. Combine butter and golden syrup in a small pan. Stir over low heat until butter has just melted; remove from heat. Pour the mixture over hazelnuts.
3 Using electric beaters, beat extra butter and syrup in a small mixing bowl until light and creamy. Add egg and ground hazelnuts, beat until well combined.

Add flour and milk all at once. Beat on low speed 1 minute, then 1 minute on high speed.
4 Spoon mixture over hazelnut base; smooth surface. Bake 35 minutes or until skewer comes out clean when inserted in centre of cake. Leave cake in tin 5 minutes before turning onto wire rack to cool. Serve warm or cool.

Orange and Currant Rock Cakes

Preparation time:
  8 minutes
Total cooking time:
  20 minutes
Makes 9 rock cakes

1 1/2 cups self-raising
  flour
1 teaspoon grated
  orange rind
60 g unsalted butter,
  melted
1/4 cup caster sugar
1/2 cup currants
1 egg, lightly beaten
2 tablespoons orange
  juice
2 teaspoons raw sugar

1 Preheat oven to moderately hot 210°C/ 190°C gas. Brush a 32 x 28 cm biscuit tray with melted butter or oil, line base with paper; grease paper.
2 Sift flour into small mixing bowl; add rind and butter. Using electric beaters, beat mixture on low speed for 2 minutes.
3 Add sugar, currants, combined egg and juice. Beat on high speed for 1 minute or until the ingredients are just combined.
4 Place 2 level tablespoons of mixture together onto prepared tray about 5 cm apart. Sprinkle rock cakes with raw sugar. Bake 20 minutes until golden brown. Turn onto wire rack to cool. Serve warm or cool with butter and marmalade, if desired.

Note: Rock cakes can also be made by rubbing butter into flour with fingertips. Add the remaining ingredients; beat with a wooden spoon for 2 minutes or until just combined. Bake as directed above.
Rock cakes can be stored up to two days in an airtight container in a cool, dry place.

Golden Syrup and Hazelnut Cake (top) and Orange and Currant Rock Cakes.

Melt & mix

The technique of melting butter and sugar together, then adding them to the flour and other dry ingredients speeds up cake-making, as it eliminates the time-consuming necessity to cream the butter and sugar. These cakes also require less beating than cakes made using the conventional method; do not overbeat.

Pineapple Streusel Cake

Preparation time:
  15 minutes
Total cooking time:
  1 hour + 10 minutes
  standing
*Makes one 23 cm
round cake*

1³/4 cups self-raising
  flour
125 g unsalted butter
²/3 cup caster sugar
2 eggs, lightly beaten
450 g can crushed
  pineapple, drained,
  ¹/2 cup juice reserved
¹/2 cup desiccated
  coconut
¹/3 cup soft brown
  sugar, firmly packed

1 Preheat oven to moderate 180°C. Brush a deep 23 cm round cake tin with melted butter or oil. Line base with paper; grease paper. Sift flour into large mixing bowl. Make a well in the centre.
2 Melt butter and sugar in a small pan over low heat, stirring until the sugar has dissolved; remove from heat. Combine eggs and reserved pineapple juice in small mixing bowl.
3 Add butter and egg mixtures to flour. Using a wooden spoon, stir until combined; do not overbeat.
4 Spoon half the mixture into prepared tin; smooth surface. Cover with combined pineapple, coconut and brown sugar. Spoon remaining batter over pineapple; smooth surface. Bake 1 hour or until skewer comes out clean when inserted in centre of cake.

*Pineapple Streusel Cake (top)
and Blueberry Muffins (page 22).*

Leave cake in the tin for 10 minutes before turning onto wire rack to cool. Serve warm or cool with whipped cream, custard or vanilla ice-cream.

Note: Arrange glacé pineapple pieces over top of cake to decorate. This cake can be stored up to two days in an airtight container in a cool, dry place.

Blueberry Muffins

Preparation time:
  15 minutes
Total cooking time:
  25 minutes
Makes 16 muffins

2 cups self-raising flour
1 cup plain flour
1 teaspoon ground
  mixed spice
1 cup blueberries
150 g unsalted butter
1 cup raw sugar
1 egg, lightly beaten
1 cup milk

1 Preheat oven to moderately hot 210°C/ 190°C gas. Brush melted butter or oil into sixteen $^1/_3$-cup capacity muffin cups. Sift flours and spice into a large mixing bowl. Add the blueberries, stir until combined. Make a well in the centre.
2 Melt butter and sugar in a small pan over low heat, stirring until sugar has dissolved; remove from heat. Combine egg and milk in a small mixing bowl.
3 Add the melted butter and egg mixtures to the dry ingredients. Using a metal spoon or fork, stir until the ingredients are combined; do not overbeat.
4 Spoon mixture into prepared muffin cups, filling two-thirds full. Bake for 25 minutes or until puffed and lightly golden. Turn onto wire rack to cool. Serve warm or cool.

Custard Butter Cake

Preparation time:
  15 minutes
Total cooking time:
  35 minutes
Makes one 20 cm square cake

1 cup self-raising
  flour
$^2/_3$ cup custard powder
$^1/_2$ teaspoon
  bicarbonate of soda
125 g unsalted butter
$^3/_4$ cup caster sugar
3 eggs, lightly beaten
$^1/_4$ cup buttermilk

1 Preheat oven to moderate 180°C. Brush a deep 20 cm square cake tin with melted butter or oil. Line base and sides with paper; grease paper.
2 Sift the flour, custard powder and soda into large mixing bowl. Make a well in the centre.
3 Melt the butter and sugar in a small pan over low heat, stirring until the sugar has dissolved; remove from heat. Combine eggs and buttermilk in a small mixing bowl. Add butter and egg mixtures to the dry ingredients. Using a wooden spoon, stir until combined; do not overbeat.
4 Spoon mixture into prepared tin; smooth surface. Bake for 35 minutes or until a skewer comes out clean when inserted in centre of cake. Turn onto wire rack to cool.

Note: Ice with Glacé or Buttercream Icing (see pages 60, 62). This cake can be stored up to four days in an airtight container.

> HINT
> For best results, muffins should be eaten on the day they are made. Store them in a cool, dry place. To serve warm, reheat in a microwave oven.

Custard Butter Cake.

Lemon and Ginger Cake

Preparation time:
  15 minutes
Total cooking time:
  50 minutes
Makes one 20 cm
round cake

2 cups self-raising
  flour
1/4 cup finely chopped
  glacé ginger
185 g unsalted butter
3/4 cup caster sugar
1 teaspoon finely grated
  lemon rind
1/4 cup lemon juice
3 eggs, lightly beaten

1 Preheat oven to
moderate 180°C. Brush
a deep 20 cm round
cake tin with melted
butter or oil. Line base
with paper; grease paper.
Sift flour into large
mixing bowl. Add glacé
ginger.
2 Make a well in the
centre. Melt butter and
sugar in a small pan
over low heat, stirring
until the sugar has
dissolved. Remove from
heat and stir in lemon
rind and juice.
3 Add butter mixture
and eggs to the dry
ingredients. Using a
wooden spoon, stir
until combined; do not
overbeat.

4 Spoon mixture into
prepared tin; smooth
surface. Bake for
50 minutes or until a
skewer comes out clean
when inserted in centre
of cake. Turn onto wire
rack to cool.

Note: Decorate cake
with Lemon Glacé Icing
(see page 62) and extra
chopped glacé ginger, if
liked. Store up to four
days in an airtight
container.

Espresso Coffee Bars

Preparation time:
  30 minutes +
  15 minutes standing
Total cooking time:
  35 minutes
Makes two 26 x 8 cm
bar cakes

1/4 cup finely ground
  espresso coffee beans
3/4 cup boiling water
2 cups self-raising flour
1/3 cup finely chopped
  pecan nuts
150 g unsalted butter
3/4 cup soft brown sugar
2 eggs, lightly beaten

1 Preheat oven to
moderate 180°C. Brush
two 26 x 8 x 4.5 cm
bar tins with melted
butter or oil. Line base
and sides with paper;

grease paper. Combine
coffee and water in a
small mixing bowl.
Allow to stand for
15 minutes. Strain,
reserve liquid, cool.
2 Sift flour into large
mixing bowl. Add
pecan nuts. Make a
well in the centre.
3 Melt butter and
sugar in a small pan
over low heat, stirring
until the sugar has
dissolved; remove from
heat. Combine eggs
with reserved coffee
liquid in a small mixing
bowl.
4 Add butter and egg
mixtures to the dry
ingredients. Using a
wooden spoon, stir
until combined; do not
overbeat.
5 Divide the mixture
evenly between the
prepared tins; smooth
surface. Bake for
35 minutes or until a
skewer comes out clean
when inserted in centre
of cake. Turn onto wire
rack to cool.

Note: One tablespoon
instant coffee powder
can be used instead of
ground coffee. Decorate
with Coffee Glacé Icing
(see page 62) and pecan
nuts, if desired.

Lemon and Ginger Cake (top) and
Espresso Coffee Bars.

Fruit and Nut Muffins

Preparation time:
15 minutes
Total cooking time:
20 minutes
Makes 12 muffins

2 cups self-raising
  flour
1 teaspoon ground
  mixed spice
1 cup chopped fruit
  medley (see Note)
*1/2 cup chopped mixed
  nuts*
125 g unsalted butter
3/4 cup caster sugar
2 eggs, lightly beaten
3/4 cup milk

1 Preheat oven to
moderately hot 210°C/
190°C gas. Brush
melted butter or oil into
twelve 1/3-cup capacity
muffin cups. Sift flour
and spice into large
mixing bowl. Add the
fruit medley and nuts,
stir until combined.
Make a well in centre.
2 Melt the butter and
sugar in a small pan
over low heat, stirring
until the sugar has
dissolved; remove from
heat. Combine eggs and
milk in a small bowl.
3 Add the butter and
egg mixtures to the dry
ingredients. Using a
metal spoon or fork,
stir until ingredients
are just combined; do
not overbeat.

4 Spoon mixture into
prepared muffin cups.
Bake 20 minutes or
until puffed and lightly
golden. Turn onto wire
rack to cool.

Note: Fruit medley is
available from health
food stores and
supermarkets. Serve
muffins warm with
butter, or ice as desired
(see pages 60–63).

Chocolate Siena Cake

Preparation time:
30 minutes
Total cooking time:
50 minutes
*Makes one 20 cm
round cake*

2/3 cup slivered almonds
*2/3 cup chopped
  macadamia nuts*
2/3 cup chopped walnuts
1 1/2 cups (180 g) mixed
  dried fruit
2/3 cup plain flour
2 tablespoons cocoa
  powder
1 teaspoon ground
  cinnamon
60 g dark chocolate,
  chopped
60 g unsalted butter
1/3 cup caster sugar
1/4 cup honey

1 Preheat oven to
moderate 180°C. Brush

a shallow 20 cm round
cake tin with melted
butter or oil. Line base
with paper; grease
paper. Combine nuts
and dried fruit in a
large mixing bowl. Add
sifted flour, cocoa and
cinnamon, stir until
combined. Make a well
in the centre.
2 Stir chocolate, butter,
sugar and honey in a
small pan over low heat
until melted and well
combined; remove from
heat.
3 Add butter mixture
to dry ingredients.
Using a wooden spoon,
stir until well combined;
do not overbeat.
4 Spoon mixture into
prepared tin; smooth
surface. Bake for
50 minutes until cake is
firm to touch in the
centre. Allow cake to
cool in the tin before
turning out. Serve cut in
thin wedges, with coffee
or liqueur.

Note: Decorate with
icing sugar or drizzle
with Glacé Icing (see
page 60) if desired.
Store in an airtight
container in a cool,
dry place.

Chocolate Siena Cake (top) and
Fruit and Nut Muffins.

Double Chocolate Cake

Preparation time:
  15 minutes
Total cooking time:
  45 minutes
Makes one 20 cm
square cake

2 cups self-raising flour
2 tablespoons cocoa
  powder
185 g unsalted butter
100 g dark chocolate,
  coarsely chopped
3/4 cup caster sugar
2 eggs, lightly beaten
1/2 cup milk

1 Preheat oven to
moderate 180°C. Brush
a deep 20 cm square
cake tin with melted
butter or oil. Line base
with paper; grease
paper. Sift flour with
cocoa into large mixing
bowl. Make a well in
the centre.
2 Stir the butter,
chocolate and sugar in
a small pan over low
heat until melted and
well combined; remove
from heat. Combine
eggs and milk in a small
mixing bowl.
3 Add the butter and
egg mixtures to the dry
ingredients. Using a
wooden spoon, stir
until just combined; do
not overbeat.

4 Spoon mixture into
prepared tin; smooth
surface. Bake for
45 minutes or until a
skewer comes out clean
when inserted in centre
of cake. Turn onto wire
rack to cool.

Note: Decorate cake
with whipped cream
and purchased
chocolates or grated
chocolate, if desired. Or
ice with Rich Chocolate
Icing (see page 63).
Store in refrigerator if
topped with cream, or
up to four days in an
airtight container.

Brandied Fruit Bars

Preparation time:
  15 minutes
Total cooking time:
  45 minutes +
  15 minutes standing
Makes two 26 x 8 cm
bar cakes

3/4 cup plain flour
1/3 cup self-raising flour
3 cups (540 g) dried
  mixed fruit
1/2 cup glacé cherries,
  halved
125 g unsalted butter
1/2 cup soft brown sugar
2 tablespoons golden
  syrup
2 eggs, lightly beaten
1/4 cup brandy

Double Chocolate Cake (top) and
Brandied Fruit Bars.

1 Preheat oven to moderate 180°C. Brush two 26 x 8 x 4.5 cm bar tins with melted butter or oil. Line base and sides with paper; grease paper. Sift flours into large mixing bowl; add mixed fruit and cherries. Make a well in the centre.
2 Melt the butter, sugar and golden syrup in a small pan over low heat, stirring until sugar has dissolved; remove from heat. Combine eggs and brandy in a small mixing bowl.
3 Add the butter and egg mixtures to the dry ingredients. Using a wooden spoon, stir until just combined; do not overbeat.
4 Spoon the mixture evenly into prepared tins; smooth surface. Bake for 45 minutes or until firm and lightly golden. Leave in tins for 15 minutes before turning onto wire rack to cool.

Note: Decorate cakes with Lemon Glacé Icing (see page 62), and extra nuts or fruit if desired. Store two weeks in an airtight container in a cool, dry place.

Rum and Raisin Cake

Preparation time:
  20 minutes
Total cooking time:
  30 minutes
Makes one 20 cm square cake

1¹/₂ cups self-raising flour
150 g unsalted butter
¹/₂ cup caster sugar
2 tablespoons dark rum
1 cup chopped raisins
3 eggs, lightly beaten
2 tablespoons milk

1 Preheat oven to moderate 180°C. Brush a 20 cm deep square cake tin with melted butter or oil. Line base and sides with paper; grease paper. Sift flour into large bowl. Make a well in the centre.
2 Melt the butter and sugar in a small pan over low heat, stirring until the sugar has dissolved; remove from heat. Stir in rum and raisins. Combine eggs and milk in small mixing bowl.
3 Add butter and egg mixtures to flour. Using a wooden spoon, stir until combined; do not overbeat.
4 Spoon the mixture into prepared tin; smooth surface. Bake 30 minutes or until a skewer comes out clean

when inserted in centre of cake. Turn onto wire rack to cool. Serve cool, sliced with butter. Store up to two days in an airtight container in a cool, dry place.

Golden Syrup and Treacle Bars

Preparation time:
  15 minutes
Total cooking time:
  30 minutes
Makes two 26 x 8 cm bar cakes

1¹/₂ cups self-raising flour
¹/₄ cup custard powder
125 g unsalted butter
¹/₄ cup golden syrup
¹/₄ cup treacle
¹/₄ cup caster sugar
2 eggs, lightly beaten
¹/₃ cup milk

1 Preheat oven to moderate 180°C. Brush two 26 x 8 x 4.5 cm bar tins with melted butter or oil. Line base and sides with paper; grease paper. Sift flour and custard powder into large bowl. Make a well in the centre.
2 Stir butter, golden syrup, treacle and sugar in a small pan over low heat until melted and well combined; remove from heat. Combine eggs and milk in a small mixing bowl.

Rum and Raisin Cake (top) and Golden Syrup and Treacle Bars.

3 Add the butter and egg mixtures to the dry ingredients. Using a wooden spoon, stir until mixture is just combined; do not overbeat.
4 Divide batter mixture evenly between the prepared tins; smooth surface. Bake for 30 minutes or until a skewer comes out clean when inserted in centre of cake. Turn onto wire rack to cool. Serve the cakes warm or cool.

Note: Decorate cakes with Buttercream Icing (see page 62); sprinkle top with ground cinnamon if desired. Store for up to two days in an airtight container in a cool, dry place.

Vanilla and Jam Cakes

Preparation time:
  20 minutes
Total cooking time:
  15 minutes
Makes 30 patty cakes

2 cups self-raising flour
150 g unsalted butter
3/4 cup caster sugar
2 eggs, lightly beaten
1/2 cup milk
2 teaspoons vanilla
  essence
1/3 cup raspberry jam

1 Preheat oven to moderate 180°C. Place 30 paper patty cases on deep patty tins or oven trays. Sift the flour into a large mixing bowl. Make a well in the centre.
2 Melt the butter and sugar in a small pan over low heat, stirring until the sugar has dissolved; remove from heat. Combine eggs, milk and essence in small mixing bowl.
3 Add butter and egg mixtures to flour. Using a wooden spoon, stir until combined; do not overbeat.
4 Place one heaped teaspoonful of mixture into each patty case. Top with 1/2 teaspoon of jam and another heaped teaspoonful of mixture. Bake for 15 minutes or until golden. Turn onto wire rack to cool. Serve cold.

Note: Decorate cakes as desired (see pages 60–63). Cakes may vary in appearance as jam may bubble to the surface. Store two days in an airtight container.

Marmalade and Coconut Crumble Cake

Preparation time:
  20 minutes
Total cooking time:
  40 minutes +
  5 minutes standing
*Makes one 20 cm
ring cake*

13/4 cups self-raising
  flour
125 g unsalted butter
3/4 cup caster sugar
2 eggs, lightly beaten
1/3 cup marmalade
1/4 cup plain yoghurt

Coconut Crumble
1/2 cup soft brown
  sugar, firmly packed
1/2 cup plain flour
1/2 cup desiccated
  coconut
90 g unsalted butter

1 Preheat oven to moderate 180°C. Brush a 20 cm ring tin with melted butter or oil. Line base with paper; grease paper. Sift flour into large bowl. Make a well in the centre.
2 Melt the butter and sugar in a small pan over low heat, stirring until the sugar has dissolved; remove from heat. Combine eggs, marmalade and yoghurt in a small mixing bowl, whisk until combined.
3 Add the butter and egg mixtures to flour. Using a wooden spoon, stir until combined; do not overbeat. Spoon mixture into prepared tin; smooth surface.
4 To make Coconut Crumble: Combine the sugar, flour and coconut in a medium mixing bowl; add butter. Using fingertips, rub butter into mixture until well combined. Sprinkle over cake batter in tin.
5 Bake 40 minutes or until skewer comes out clean when inserted in centre of cake. Leave cake in tin 5 minutes before turning onto wire rack to cool. Serve warm or cold, with whipped cream or vanilla ice-cream.

Note: Store this cake for up to three days in an airtight container. Cake can be reheated in the microwave oven.

Marmalade and Coconut Crumble Cake (top) and Vanilla and Jam Cakes.

Sprinkle brown sugar evenly over base of tin. Cut pears in half and arrange in tin.

Heat butter and sugar in a small pan until butter is melted and sugar dissolved.

Pear Upside-down Cake

Preparation time:
  15 minutes
Total cooking time:
  50 minutes +
  15 minutes standing
*Makes one 21 x 14 cm
loaf cake*

2 tablespoons soft
  brown sugar
425 g can pear halves
  in syrup
2 cups self-raising flour
125 g unsalted butter
³/4 cup caster sugar
2 eggs, lightly beaten

1 Preheat oven to
moderate 180°C. Brush
a 21 x 14 x 7 cm loaf
tin with melted butter
or oil. Line base and
sides with paper; grease
paper. Sprinkle brown
sugar evenly over base
of tin. Drain pears,
reserving syrup. Cut
pears in half, arrange
over base of tin.
2 Sift flour into a large
mixing bowl. Make a
well in the centre.
3 Melt butter and
sugar in a small pan
over low heat, stirring
until the sugar has
dissolved; remove from
heat. Combine eggs and
reserved syrup.
4 Add butter and egg
mixtures to flour. Using
a wooden spoon, stir
until combined; do not
overbeat.
5 Spoon mixture over
pears; smooth surface.
Bake 50 minutes or
until skewer comes out
clean when inserted in
centre of cake. Leave
cake in tin 15 minutes
before turning onto
wire rack to cool.

Note: Be sure to allow
the full standing time
before turning out, or
the pears may not
adhere to the cake.

Pear Upside-down Cake.

*Add melted butter mixture and lightly
beaten eggs to flour.*

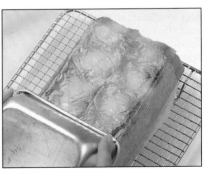

*Leave cake in tin for 15 minutes, then
turn onto a wire rack to cool.*

Apricot Nectar Cake

Preparation time:
  15 minutes
Total cooking time:
  40 minutes
Makes one 23 cm ring cake

1½ cups self-raising
  flour
½ cup desiccated
  coconut
125 g unsalted butter
1 cup caster sugar
2 eggs, lightly beaten
1 cup apricot nectar
½ cup sour cream

1 Preheat oven to moderate 180°C. Brush a 23 cm deep baba tin with melted butter or oil. Coat base and sides evenly with flour; shake off excess. Sift flour into large mixing bowl. Add desiccated coconut. Make a well in the centre of the mixture.
2 Melt butter and sugar in a small pan over low heat, stirring until the sugar has dissolved; remove from heat. Combine eggs, apricot nectar and sour cream in a medium mixing bowl.
3 Add butter and egg mixtures to flour. Using a wooden spoon, stir until combined; do not overbeat.
4 Spoon mixture into prepared tin; smooth

surface. Bake for 40 minutes or until a skewer comes out clean when inserted in centre of cake. Turn onto wire rack to cool. Serve warm or cool.

Note: Decorate cake with Orange, Lemon or Passionfruit Glacé Icing (see page 62), if desired. Store up to three days in an airtight container in a cool dry place.

Hot Apple Cake

Preparation time:
  20 minutes
Total cooking time:
  1 hour
Makes one 23 cm round cake

1½ cups self-raising
  flour
½ cup plain flour
185 g unsalted butter
⅔ cup caster sugar
3 eggs, lightly beaten
⅓ cup milk
1 cup pie apple
2 tablespoons golden
  syrup
1 teaspoon cinnamon
  sugar, optional

1 Preheat oven to a moderate 180°C. Brush a deep 23 cm round cake tin with melted butter or oil. Line base with paper; grease paper. Sift flours into large mixing bowl. Make a well in the centre.
2 Melt the butter and sugar in a small pan over low heat, stirring until the sugar has dissolved; remove from heat. Combine eggs and milk in small bowl.
3 Add butter and egg mixtures to flour. Using a wooden spoon, stir until just combined; do not overbeat.
4 Pour half the mixture into the prepared tin; smooth surface. Top with pie apple, drizzle with golden syrup. Spoon remaining cake mixture over; smooth surface. Sprinkle with cinnamon sugar if liked. Bake 1 hour or until skewer comes out clean when inserted in centre of cake. Turn out, dust with icing sugar if liked and serve immediately with cream or ice-cream.

Note: Substitute 1 cup of freshly cooked apple for pie apple, if liked. Add a clove or a pinch of cinnamon to the apple for extra flavour.

Apricot Nectar Cake (top) and Hot Apple Cake.

Food processor cakes

The food processor has made quite a difference in the kitchens of modern cooks. The heavy duty motor can combine the ingredients for a cake in a matter of seconds and for this reason it is important not to overbeat the cake mixture – process only until the ingredients are combined and smooth. Our grandmothers could only have dreamt about a machine that would help them turn out light and lovely cakes so quickly and easily.

Quick Butter Cake

Preparation time:
10 minutes
Total cooking time:
45 minutes +
5 minutes standing
Makes one 23 cm ring cake

1¹/2 cups self-raising
  flour
150 g unsalted butter,
  chopped
³/4 cup caster sugar
2 eggs, lightly beaten
¹/2 cup buttermilk
2 teaspoons vanilla
  essence

1 Preheat oven to moderate 180°C. Brush a 23 cm baba tin with melted butter or oil.

2 Place flour, butter pieces and sugar in food processor bowl. Using the pulse action, process for 20 seconds or until mixture is fine and crumbly. Add the combined eggs, buttermilk and vanilla to bowl, process for 10 seconds or until the mixture is smooth.

3 Spoon into prepared tin; smooth surface. Bake 45 minutes or until a skewer comes out clean when inserted in centre of cake. Leave in tin 5 minutes; turn onto wire rack to cool.

Note: Decorate with Glacé or Rich Chocolate Icing (see pages 60 and 63). Store up to three days in an airtight container.

Quick Butter Cake (top) and
Apple Cardamom Cake (see page 40).

Apple Cardamom Cake

Preparation time:
8 minutes
Total cooking time:
40 minutes +
5 minutes standing
Makes one 20 cm round cake

185 g unsalted butter, chopped
1 teaspoon vanilla essence
3/4 cup caster sugar
3 eggs
1 green apple, peeled and chopped
1/3 cup coarsely chopped dried apples
1/4 cup whole almond kernels
1/4 teaspoon ground cardamom
2 cups self-raising flour
1/3 cup milk

1 Preheat oven to moderate 180°C. Brush a deep 20 cm round tin with melted butter or oil.
2 Place butter, essence, sugar and eggs in food processor bowl. Using pulse action, process for 1 minute or until mixture is light and creamy. Add apples, almonds and cardamom to bowl; process for 15 seconds. Add flour and milk; process 20 seconds or until apple and almonds are finely chopped and mixture is thick and almost smooth.
3 Pour the mixture evenly into prepared tin; smooth surface. Bake for 40 minutes or until skewer comes out clean when inserted in centre of cake. Leave cake in tin 5 minutes before turning onto wire rack to cool. Decorate with Glacé Icing (see page 60).

Chocolate Sour Cream Cake

Preparation time:
10 minutes
Total cooking time:
45 minutes
Makes one 23 cm baba cake

11/2 cups self-raising flour
1/2 cup cocoa powder
1 teaspoon bicarbonate of soda
125 g unsalted butter, chopped
1 cup caster sugar
4 eggs, lightly beaten
3/4 cup sour cream

1 Preheat oven to moderate 180°C. Brush a 23 cm baba tin with melted butter or oil.
2 Place the flour, cocoa and soda in food processor bowl; add butter and sugar. Using pulse action, process for 20 seconds or until mixture is fine and crumbly. Add combined eggs and sour cream to bowl, process for 10 seconds or until the mixture is smooth.
3 Spoon into prepared tin; smooth surface. Bake 45 minutes or until skewer comes out clean when inserted in centre of cake. Turn onto wire rack to cool. Ice with Chocolate Glacé or Rich Chocolate Icing (see pages 62, 63).

Note: Buttermilk or milk can be used instead of sour cream. This cake can be stored up to three days in an airtight container.

Coconut Nutmeg Cake

Preparation time:
15 minutes
Total cooking time:
1 hour
Makes one 23 cm round cake

11/2 cups self-raising flour
1 teaspoon ground nutmeg
125 g unsalted butter, chopped
1 cup caster sugar
4 eggs, lightly beaten
1 cup milk
2 teaspoons finely grated lemon rind
1/4 cup lemon juice
1 cup desiccated coconut

Chocolate Sour Cream Cake (top) and Coconut Nutmeg Cake.

1 Preheat oven to moderate 180°C. Brush a deep 23 cm round cake tin with melted butter or oil. Line base with paper; grease paper.
2 Place flour, nutmeg, butter and sugar in food processor. Using pulse action, process for 20 seconds or until mixture is fine and crumbly. Add combined eggs, milk, lemon rind and juice, process for 10 seconds or until mixture is smooth. Transfer to large mixing bowl. Fold in coconut.
3 Spoon mixture into prepared tin; smooth surface. Bake 1 hour or until skewer comes out clean when inserted in centre of cake. Turn onto wire rack to cool. Decorate with Buttercream or Cream Cheese Icing (see pages 62 and 63).

41

Pumpkin Prune Loaf

Preparation time:
  20 minutes
Total cooking time:
  1 hour + 5 minutes
  standing
Makes one 21 x 14 cm loaf

2 cups self-raising flour
1 teaspoon ground
  cinnamon
125 g unsalted butter,
  chopped
1 cup soft brown sugar,
  firmly packed
3 eggs, lightly beaten
1 cup cold mashed
  pumpkin (300 g raw
  pumpkin)
1/2 cup desiccated
  coconut
1/2 cup chopped, pitted
  prunes

1 Preheat oven to
moderate 180°C. Brush
a 21 x 14 x 7 cm loaf
tin with melted butter or
oil. Line base and sides
with paper; grease paper.
2 Place flour and
cinnamon in food
processor bowl; add
butter and sugar. Using
pulse action, process
20 seconds or until
mixture is fine and
crumbly. Add combined
eggs and pumpkin to
bowl, process 10 seconds
or until smooth.

3 Transfer mixture to
large bowl. Using a
metal spoon, fold in
coconut and prunes.
Spoon mixture into the
prepared tin; smooth
surface. Bake 1 hour or
until skewer comes out
clean when inserted in
centre of loaf. Leave
loaf in tin for 5 minutes
before turning onto
wire rack to cool.

Note: Decorate with
Buttercream Icing (see
page 62), if liked.

Cinnamon Nut Cake

Preparation time:
  20 minutes
Total cooking time:
  1 hour + 5 minutes
  standing
*Makes one 20 cm
square cake*

1 1/4 cups self-raising
  flour
125 g unsalted butter,
  chopped
1 cup caster sugar
2 eggs, lightly beaten
1/2 cup sour cream
1 teaspoon vanilla
  essence
1/2 cup finely chopped
  hazelnuts
1/4 cup soft brown
  sugar, firmly packed
1 1/2 teaspoons ground
  cinnamon

*Pumpkin Prune Loaf (top) and
Cinnamon Nut Cake.*

1 Preheat oven to
moderate 180°C. Brush
a 20 cm square cake tin
with melted butter or
oil. Line base with
paper; grease paper.
2 Place flour in food
processor bowl; add
butter and caster sugar.
Using pulse action,
process for 20 seconds
or until mixture is fine
and crumbly. Add
combined eggs, sour
cream and essence to
bowl, process for
10 seconds or until the
mixture is smooth.
3 Combine hazelnuts,
brown sugar and
cinnamon in a small
mixing bowl. Spoon
half the cake mixture
into the prepared tin;
smooth surface.
Sprinkle with half the
hazelnut mixture.
Spoon over remaining
cake mixture; smooth
surface. Sprinkle with
remaining hazelnut
mixture. Bake 1 hour
or until skewer comes
out clean when inserted
in centre of cake. Leave
in tin 5 minutes before
turning onto wire rack
to cool. Serve warm or
cold with cream.

Note: This cake can be
stored up to four days
in an airtight container.

Place butter, sugar, chopped lime and lemon and egg into food processor bowl.

Spoon the batter mixture into the prepared tin and smooth the surface.

Lemon-lime Coconut Cake

Preparation time:
8 minutes
Total cooking time:
45 minutes
*Makes one 20 cm
square cake*

125 g unsalted butter
2/3 cup caster sugar
1/2 small unpeeled
  lemon, chopped
1/2 unpeeled lime,
  chopped
1 egg
2/3 cup coconut cream
1/2 cup fine ground
  semolina
1/2 cup self-raising flour
1/2 cup wholemeal self-
  raising flour

1 Preheat oven to moderate 180°C. Brush a shallow 20 cm square cake tin with melted butter or oil, line base with paper; grease paper.

2 Place butter, sugar, chopped lemon and lime and egg into food processor bowl. Using pulse action, process for 30 seconds. Add cream and semolina to bowl, process for 15 seconds. Add the flours, process for 15 seconds or until all the ingredients are combined and mixture is smooth.

3 Spoon the mixture evenly into prepared tin; smooth surface. Bake for 45 minutes or until a skewer comes out clean when inserted in centre of cake. Turn cake onto wire rack to cool.

Note: Brush cake with Fruit Glaze or ice with Cream Cheese Icing (see page 63) and purchased lemon jellies if desired. Store up to two days in an airtight container, in a cool, dark place.

Lemon-lime Coconut Cake.

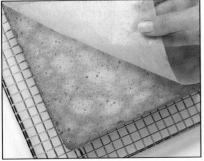

Turn cake onto wire rack to cool. Peel off the paper on the base of cake.

Brush cake with warmed apricot jam glaze (optional, see page 63).

Apricot Cake

Preparation time:
20 minutes
Total cooking time:
1 hour + 5 minutes
standing
*Makes one 20 cm
round cake*

1 cup finely chopped
  dried apricots
1/4 cup boiling water
2 cups self-raising flour
125 g unsalted butter,
  chopped
3/4 cup caster sugar
2 eggs, lightly beaten
1/2 cup apricot nectar

1 Preheat oven to
moderate 180°C. Brush
a 20 cm round cake tin
with melted butter or
oil. Line base with
paper; grease paper.
2 Combine apricots
and water in a large
mixing bowl. Stand
10 minutes or until
water has been absorbed.
3 Place flour, butter
and sugar in food
processor bowl. Using
pulse action, process
for 20 seconds or until
mixture is fine and
crumbly. Add combined
eggs and nectar to bowl,
process 10 seconds or
until mixture is smooth.
Add to bowl of apricots.
Using a metal spoon,
stir until just combined;
do not overbeat.
4 Spoon mixture into
prepared tin; smooth

surface. Bake 1 hour or
until skewer comes out
clean when inserted in
centre of cake. Leave
cake in tin 5 minutes
before turning onto
wire rack to cool.

Note: Decorate cake
with Orange or Lemon
Glacé Icing (see page
62) or sifted icing sugar,
if desired. Store up to
three days in an airtight
container.

Chocolate Walnut Cake

Preparation time:
15 minutes
Total cooking time:
55 minutes +
  5 minutes standing
*Makes one 28 x 18 cm
cake*

200 g unsalted butter
150 g dark chocolate,
  chopped
1 1/2 cups self-raising
  flour
3/4 cup caster sugar
2 eggs, lightly beaten
3/4 cup milk
1/2 cup chopped
  walnuts

1 Preheat oven to
moderate 180°C.
Brush a shallow
28 x 18 cm oblong
cake tin with melted
butter or oil. Line base
and sides with paper;
grease paper.
2 Place butter and
chocolate in a small
pan. Stir over low heat
until melted and
mixture is combined;
remove from heat.
3 Place flour, butter
mixture, sugar, eggs
and milk in food
processor bowl. Using
the pulse action,
process for 20 seconds
or until the mixture is
smooth. Transfer
mixture to large
mixing bowl. Using a
metal spoon, fold in
walnuts.
4 Spoon mixture into
prepared tin; smooth
surface. Bake for
55 minutes or until
skewer comes out
clean when inserted in
centre of cake. Leave
cake in tin 5 minutes
before turning onto
wire rack to cool.

Note: Decorate with
Buttercream or Rich
Chocolate Icing (see
pages 62 and 63), if
desired. This cake may
be stored up to three
days in an airtight
container in a cool
dry place.

*Apricot Cake (top) and
Chocolate Walnut Cake.*

Banana Spice Loaf

Preparation time:
15 minutes
Total cooking time:
1 hour + 5 minutes
standing
*Makes one 21 x 14 cm
loaf*

1 1/2 *cups self-raising
flour*
1 *teaspoon ground
mixed spice*
125 *g unsalted butter,
chopped*
3/4 *cup caster sugar*
2 *eggs, lightly beaten*
1/3 *cup plain yoghurt*
2/3 *cup mashed ripe
banana*

1 Preheat oven to
moderate 180°C. Brush
a 21 x 14 x 7 cm loaf
tin with melted butter
or oil. Line base and
sides with paper; grease
paper.
2 Place flour, spice,
butter and sugar in
food processor bowl.
Using pulse action,
process for 20 seconds
or until mixture is fine
and crumbly. Add
combined eggs, yoghurt
and banana, process
10 seconds or until
mixture is just combined;
do not overbeat.
3 Spoon mixture into
prepared tin; smooth
surface. Bake 1 hour or
until skewer comes out
clean when inserted in
centre of cake. Leave

cake in tin 5 minutes
before turning onto
wire rack to cool.
Decorate with Lemon
Glacé or Buttercream
Icing (see page 62).

Note: Do not overbeat
mixture once bananas
have been added or
cake may be coarse and
heavy in texture.

Cardamom Honey
Ring

Preparation time:
10 minutes
Total cooking time:
35 minutes +
5 minutes standing
*Makes one 20 cm
ring cake*

2 *cups self-raising flour*
1 *teaspoon ground
cardamom*
1/2 *teaspoon ground
cinnamon*
125 *g unsalted butter,
chopped*
2/3 *cup raw sugar*
2 *eggs, lightly beaten*
1/2 *cup milk*
1/4 *cup honey*

1 Preheat oven to
moderate 180°C. Brush
a 20 cm ring tin with
melted butter or oil.
Line base with paper;
grease paper.
2 Place flour, cardamom
and cinnamon in food
processor bowl; add
butter and sugar. Using
pulse action, process

20 seconds or until
mixture is fine and
crumbly. Add combined
eggs, milk and honey to
bowl, process for
10 seconds or until the
mixture is smooth.
3 Spoon mixture into
prepared tin; smooth
surface. Bake for
35 minutes or until
skewer comes out clean
when inserted in centre
of cake. Leave cake in
tin 5 minutes before
turning onto wire rack
to cool.

Note: Decorate with
Honey Buttercream
Icing (see page 62).
Store up to three days
in an airtight container.

Chocolate Almond
Cakes

Preparation time:
15 minutes
Total cooking time:
15 minutes
Makes 24 patty cakes

1 1/4 *cups self-raising
flour*
2 *tablespoons cocoa
powder*
125 *g unsalted butter,
chopped*
1/3 *cup caster sugar*
2 *eggs, lightly beaten*
1/2 *cup buttermilk*
1 *tablespoon golden
syrup*
1/3 *cup flaked almonds*
50 *g dark chocolate,
melted, to decorate*

Clockwise from top: Cardamom Honey Ring, Banana Spice Loaf and Chocolate Almond Cakes.

1 Preheat oven to moderate 180°C. Brush 24 shallow patty cake tins with melted butter or oil.
2 Place flour, cocoa, butter and sugar in food processor bowl. Using the pulse action, process 20 seconds or until mixture is fine and crumbly. Add combined eggs, buttermilk and syrup to bowl, process 10 seconds or until the mixture is smooth.
3 Divide flaked almonds evenly between patty tins. Spoon mixture over almonds, filling cups two-thirds full. Bake 15 minutes or until firm. Turn onto wire rack to cool. Pipe spirals of melted chocolate onto cakes and serve.

49

Easy Orange Loaf

Preparation time:
  15 minutes
Total cooking time:
  50 minutes +
  5 minutes standing
*Makes one 21 x 14 cm
loaf cake*

1¼ *cups self-raising
  flour*
125 *g unsalted butter,
  chopped*
⅔ *cup caster sugar*
3 *eggs, lightly beaten*
⅓ *cup buttermilk*
2 *teaspoons finely
  grated orange rind*

1 Preheat oven to
moderate 180°C. Brush
a 21 x 14 x 7 cm loaf
tin with melted butter or
oil. Line base and sides
with paper; grease paper.
2 Place flour, butter
and sugar in food
processor bowl. Using
the pulse action,
process 20 seconds or
until mixture is fine and
crumbly. Add combined
eggs, buttermilk and
rind to bowl, process
for 10 seconds or until
the mixture is smooth.
3 Spoon the mixture
into the prepared tin;
smooth surface. Bake
50 minutes or until a
skewer comes out clean
when inserted in centre
of cake. Leave cake in
tin 5 minutes before
turning onto a wire
rack to cool.

Note: Milk, sour cream
or yoghurt can be used
instead of buttermilk in
this recipe. Decorate
cake with Orange or
Lemon Buttercream
(see page 62) and
purchased orange
sweets, if desired. Store
up to three days in an
airtight container in a
cool dry place.

Almond and Semolina Cake

Preparation time:
  15 minutes
Total cooking time:
  1 hour + 5 minutes
  standing
*Makes one 20 cm
round cake*

1 *cup self-raising
  flour*
⅔ *cup ground almonds*
⅔ *cup semolina*
125 *g unsalted butter,
  chopped*
1 *cup caster sugar*
2 *eggs, lightly beaten*
½ *cup milk*
2 *teaspoons finely
  grated orange rind*
¼ *cup orange juice*

1 Preheat oven to
moderate 180°C. Brush
a deep 20 cm round
cake tin with melted
butter or oil. Line base
with paper; grease paper.
2 Place flour, almonds,
semolina, butter and
sugar in food processor
bowl. Using the pulse
action, process for
20 seconds or until the
mixture is fine and
crumbly. Add combined
eggs, milk, orange rind
and juice to bowl,
process 10 seconds or
until combined.
3 Spoon the mixture
into prepared tin;
smooth surface. Bake
for 1 hour or until a
skewer comes out clean
when inserted in centre
of cake. Leave the cake
in the tin 5 minutes
before turning onto
wire rack to cool. Serve
warm or cool.

Note: Ground almonds
and semolina give the
raw mixture a rough
texture in this cake. The
cooked cake will have a
slightly crunchy texture.
Decorate finished cake
with Glacé, Buttercream
or Cream Cheese Icing
(see pages 60–63) and
orange rind or toasted
flaked almonds if
desired. Store cake for
up to two days in an
airtight container in a
cool, dry place.

*Almond and Semolina Cake (top)
and Easy Orange Loaf.*

Packet mix cakes

Cakes made with a packet mix as their base can be deliciously country plain or all-dressed-up for dessert. For best results, choose a packet mix with a content of only 30 or 40 grams more or less than the weight given in each recipe in this section.

Chocolate Strawberry Gateau

Preparation time:
 9 minutes
Total cooking time:
 35 minutes
Makes one 23 cm round sandwich cake

510 g packet
 SuperMoist Chocolate
 Fudge cake mix
2 eggs
1 cup water
1/2 cup oil
2/3 cup cream
2 tablespoons icing
 sugar, sifted
1 cup (180 g) thinly
 sliced strawberries
whole strawberries, to
 decorate

1 Preheat oven to moderate 180°C. Brush two deep 23 cm round cake tins with melted butter or oil, line base with paper; grease paper.

2 Place contents of packet mix, eggs, water and oil in large mixing bowl. Using electric beaters, beat ingredients together on medium speed for 1 minute or until just combined. Beat for 2 minutes on high speed or until mixture is smooth.

3 Divide the mixture evenly between the prepared tins; smooth surface. Bake for 35 minutes or until a skewer comes out clean when inserted in centre of cake. Turn cakes onto wire rack to cool.

4 Using electric beaters, beat cream and icing sugar in small mixing bowl until stiff peaks form. When cake is cool, spread cream over one layer. Arrange the sliced strawberries over cream; top with other cake layer. Decorate with whole strawberries and chocolates, if liked.

Chocolate Strawberry Gateau (top) and Mocha Ring Cake (see page 54).

Mocha Ring Cake

Preparation time:
  10 minutes
Total cooking time:
  35 minutes
*Makes one 20 cm
ring cake*

370 g packet Swiss Milk
  Chocolate cake mix
2 eggs, lightly beaten
1/4 cup strong black coffee
1/2 cup cream
60 g white chocolate,
  finely chopped

1 Preheat oven to
moderate 180°C. Brush
a 20 cm ring tin with
melted butter or oil,
line base with paper;
grease paper.
2 Place contents of
packet mix, eggs,
coffee, cream and
chocolate into a small
mixing bowl. Using
electric beaters, beat
ingredients together on
low speed for 1 minute
or until just combined.
Beat 2 minutes on
medium speed or until
mixture is smooth.
3 Spoon mixture into
the prepared tin;
smooth surface. Bake
for 35 minutes or until
a skewer comes out
clean when inserted in
centre of cake. Turn
onto wire rack to cool.
Ice with Coffee Glacé
Icing and decorate with
white chocolate curls
and chocolates.

Apple Tea Cake

Preparation time:
  15 minutes
Total cooking time:
  30 minutes +
  5 minutes standing
*Makes one 20 cm
round cake*

210 g packet French
  Tea Cake mix
20 g unsalted butter,
  softened
1 egg
1/3 cup sparkling apple
  juice
1/2 cup finely chopped
  green apple
cinnamon topping
  sachet
1 tablespoon desiccated
  coconut
20 g unsalted butter,
  extra, melted
2 tablespoons flaked
  almonds

1 Preheat oven to
moderate 180°C. Brush
a shallow 20 cm round
cake tin with melted
butter or oil. Line base
with paper; grease paper.
2 Reserve 2 tablespoons
of the tea cake mix for
topping. Place the
remaining contents of
packet mix into small
mixing bowl with
butter, egg, juice and
apple. Using electric
beaters, beat ingredients
together on low speed
for 2 minutes, or until
mixture is smooth.
Spread mixture over
base of prepared tin;
smooth surface.
3 Place cinnamon
topping, reserved cake
mix, coconut and extra
butter in small mixing
bowl. Using fingertips,
rub butter into mixture
for 1 minute or until
mixture is a coarse,
crumbly texture; add
almonds. Sprinkle the
mixture over cake
batter, bake 30 minutes
or until skewer comes
out clean when inserted
in centre of cake. Leave
cake in tin 5 minutes
before turning onto
wire rack to cool. Dust
with icing sugar and
serve warm or cold
with custard or cream.

Peach and
Zucchini Muffins

Preparation time:
  8 minutes
Total cooking time:
  18 minutes +
  5 minutes standing
Makes 15 muffins

340 g packet Golden
  Buttercake mix
1 egg
2 teaspoons grated
  lemon rind
2/3 cup coarsely grated
  zucchini
1/2 cup finely chopped
  canned peaches in
  natural juice, well
  drained
60 g unsalted butter,
  melted

Apple Tea Cake (top) and Peach and Zucchini Muffins.

1 Preheat oven to moderately hot 210°C/190°C gas. Brush melted butter or oil into fifteen ⅓-cup capacity muffin cups.
2 Place contents of the packet mix, egg, rind, zucchini, peaches and butter in large bowl. Using a wooden spoon, stir until the ingredients are just combined; do not overbeat.
3 Spoon mixture into prepared muffin cups, filling two-thirds full. Bake 18 minutes or until puffed and lightly browned. Leave in tin for 5 minutes before turning onto wire rack to cool. Decorate with Buttercream or Cream Cheese Icing (see pages 62–63) and extra fresh peach slices, if liked.

55

Honey Date Cake

Preparation time:
10 minutes
Total cooking time:
35 minutes +
10 minutes standing
Makes one 20 cm
round cake

340 g packet Golden
  Buttercake cake mix
1/2 cup (120 g) finely
  chopped fresh dates
1 teaspoon mixed spice
1 egg
1/2 cup buttermilk
1/4 cup honey
20 g unsalted butter
1 tablespoon water

1 Preheat oven to
moderate 180°C. Brush
a shallow 20 cm round
cake tin with melted
butter or oil, line base
and sides with paper;
grease paper.
2 Place contents of
packet mix, dates,
mixed spice, egg and
buttermilk in a small
mixing bowl. Using
electric beaters, beat
ingredients together on
low speed for 1 minute
or until just combined.
Beat 2 minutes on
medium speed or until
mixture is smooth.
3 Spread mixture into
prepared tin. Bake for
35 minutes or until a
skewer comes out clean
when inserted in centre.
Leave cake in tin for
10 minutes before
carefully lifting onto
a wire rack.
4 Combine honey,
butter and water in a
small pan. Stir over low
heat 1 minute or until
butter has just melted.
Brush warm honey
mixture over warm
cake. Serve warm with
custard or ice-cream.

Note: Decorate cake
with sifted icing sugar,
if desired.

Honey Date Cake.

Remove and discard seeds from fresh
dates. Chop dates finely.

Place content: of packet mix, dates, spice,
egg and buttermilk in a small bowl.

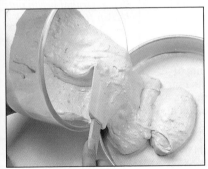

Using a spatula, spread mixture evenly into the prepared tin.

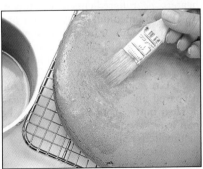

Using a pastry brush, brush warm honey mixture over cake.

Caramel Crunch Cake

Preparation time:
  8 minutes
Total cooking time:
  35 minutes
Makes one 20 cm round cake

225 g packet
  Butterscotch Sponge
  Pudding mix
2 eggs, lightly beaten
1/4 cup water
1/4 cup oil
2 tablespoons unsalted
  butter
1/4 cup soft brown sugar
2 cups cornflakes,
  lightly crushed

1 Preheat oven to moderate 180°C. Brush a shallow 20 cm round cake tin with melted butter or oil, line base with paper; grease paper.
2 Place contents of packet mix, eggs, water and oil in small mixing bowl. Using electric beaters, beat ingredients together on medium speed 3 minutes or until mixture is smooth, scraping down side of bowl occasionally. Pour the mixture into the prepared tin.
3 Heat butter in small pan over low heat until just melted; remove from heat. Stir in brown sugar and cornflakes.
4 Spoon the mixture evenly over cake batter.

Bake 35 minutes or until skewer comes out clean when inserted in centre of cake. Invert onto wire rack to cool.

Choc-chip Banana Nut Bars

Preparation time:
  8 minutes
Total cooking time:
  25 minutes
Makes two 26 x 8 cm bar cakes

310 g packet Banana
  cake mix
1/2 cup mashed banana
2 eggs, lightly beaten
1 tablespoon crunchy
  peanut butter
1/4 cup chopped nuts
1/3 cup choc bits

1 Preheat oven to moderate 180°C. Brush two 26 x 8 x 4.5 cm bar tins with melted butter or oil. Cover base with paper, extending over two sides; grease paper.
2 Place contents of packet mix, banana, eggs, peanut butter, nuts and choc bits into a small mixing bowl. Using electric beaters, beat ingredients together on medium speed for 3 minutes or until the mixture is smooth,

scraping down side of bowl occasionally.
3 Divide mixture evenly between the prepared tins; smooth surface. Bake for 25 minutes or until a skewer comes out clean when inserted in centre of cakes. Turn onto wire rack to cool. Decorate as desired or serve sliced, with butter.

Orange Pecan Cake

Preparation time:
  12 minutes
Total cooking time:
  35 minutes +
  5 minutes standing
Makes one 20 cm square cake

350 g packet Orange
  cake mix
2 teaspoons grated
  orange rind
1/4 cup sour cream
1/2 cup vegetable oil
1/3 cup water
1/3 cup ground pecan nuts
1/3 cup finely chopped
  pecan nuts

1 Preheat oven to moderate 180°C. Brush a shallow 20 cm square cake tin with melted butter or oil, line base with paper; grease paper.
2 Place contents of packet mix, orange rind, sour cream, oil, water and ground pecan nuts into small

Clockwise from top left, Caramel Crunch Cake, Choc-chip Banana Nut Bar and Orange Pecan Cake.

mixing bowl. Using electric beaters, beat the ingredients together on medium speed for 3 minutes or until the mixture is smooth, scraping down side of bowl occasionally.

3 Pour mixture into prepared tin; smooth surface. Sprinkle the chopped nuts over cake batter, press lightly into the mixture.

4 Bake for 35 minutes or until skewer comes out clean when inserted in centre of cake. Leave cake in tin 5 minutes before inverting onto a wire rack to cool. Dust lightly with icing sugar to serve, if liked. Serve warm or cold.

Icings

The icing on the cake is, to some people, as important as the cake itself! The plainest cake can be transformed into a work of art by a drift of icing sugar or an imaginative decoration. This guide illustrates quick, simple and delicious cake toppings, and recommends some ready-made sweets and other ideas for finishing off your cake in style – fast.

For decorating cakes in a hurry:

✿ Whip cream to firm peaks, pipe or spread over cake. Top with chocolate flakes (made by gently crumbling a flaked chocolate bar).

✿ Pile the centre of a plain sponge with fresh berries, pipe swirls of whipped cream around the edge.

✿ Sift icing sugar over cakes using strips of paper or through a lace doily to create striking patterns. Icing sugar can be plain, or mixed with cocoa, drinking chocolate or cinnamon. Place in a small metal strainer and scrape with a spoon to achieve a fine drift of sugar.

✿ Purchased sweets such as marzipan fruits, after-dinner mints, small discs or squares of chocolate or foil-covered chocolate money (wrapped and unwrapped) positioned on chocolate glacé icing turn an everyday cake into a celebration cake.

✿ Drizzle or pipe melted white or dark chocolate (or both) over iced or un-iced cakes.

✿ Sprinkle chopped, toasted nuts, chocolate or coloured sprinkles over icing.

✿ Edge iced cake with whole nuts or glacé cherries.

The following recipes are for classic cake toppings with variations in flavour. Glacé, Buttercream and Cream Cheese Icings will give the finishing touch to your cakes easily and quickly. Choose your own or follow the suggestions given after the recipes.

Glacé Icing

This is a shiny, smooth icing made with icing sugar, a small amount of butter and a little fruit juice or other flavourings such as coffee or chocolate, so it can be either tangy or sweet. The mixture is combined over gently simmering water (do not overheat or icing will become dull, flat and grainy) and spread with a wide knife. Dip the knife into hot water occasionally to give a smooth, shiny finish. Glacé Icing can be drizzled over the cake in a decorative pattern. This quantity makes enough to cover the top of a 20 cm round or square cake.

1. Combine icing sugar, butter, lemon juice.

2. Spread Glacé Icing with a flat knife.

Many kinds of sweets can be used to make a cake into something special.

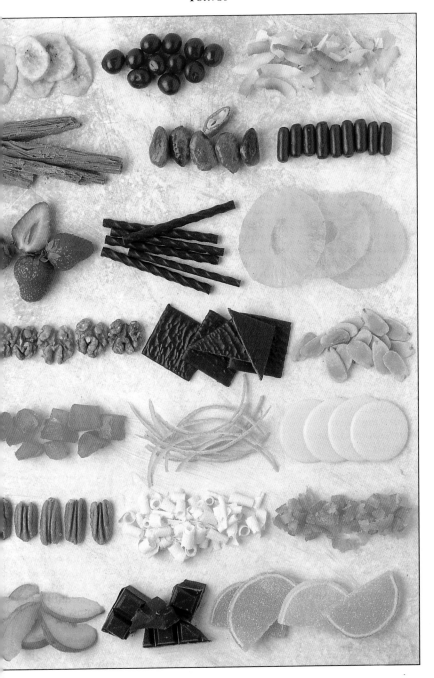

Lemon Glacé
1 cup icing sugar
1 teaspoon finely grated lemon rind
10 g unsalted butter
1–2 tablespoons lemon juice

Orange Glacé
1 cup icing sugar
1 teaspoon finely grated lemon rind
10 g unsalted butter
1–2 tablespoons orange juice

Passionfruit Glacé
1 cup icing sugar
10 g unsalted butter
1–2 tablespoons passionfruit pulp

Coffee Glacé
1 cup icing sugar
1 teaspoon instant coffee powder
10 g unsalted butter
1–2 tablespoons water

Chocolate Glacé
1 cup icing sugar
1 tablespoon cocoa powder
10 g unsalted butter
1–2 tablespoons hot milk

Glacé Icing method
Combine sifted icing sugar, flavouring, butter and sufficient liquid in a small heatproof bowl to form a firm paste. Stand bowl over pan of simmering water and stir until icing is smooth and glossy; remove from heat. Using a wide knife, spread icing over cake.

Buttercream Icing
This icing is rich and creamy, with a substantial amount of butter used in the mixture. Have the butter at room temperature for easier mixing. Icing can be spread smoothly, swirled with a knife for a textured effect or first smoothed then run through with a fork. Use a generous layer of icing for the best flavour and appearance. This amount makes enough to cover the top of a 20 cm round or square cake. Double the quantity if you want to ice the sides or layer the cake with icing. This icing goes well with cakes such as sour cream, vegetable or banana cakes.

1. *Beat butter and sugar; add cocoa powder.*

2. *Spread in a generous layer over cake.*

Honey Buttercream
60 g unsalted butter
1/3 cup icing sugar
2–3 teaspoons honey

Chocolate Buttercream
60 g unsalted butter
1/2 cup icing sugar
2 tablespoons cocoa powder
2 teaspoons milk

Rich Chocolate Buttercream
60 g unsalted butter
1/3 cup icing sugar
60 g dark chocolate, melted

Lemon Buttercream
60 g unsalted butter
1/3 cup icing sugar
2 teaspoons finely grated lemon rind

Orange Buttercream
60 g unsalted butter
1/3 cup icing sugar
2 teaspoons finely grated orange rind

Buttercream method
Using electric beaters, beat butter and sifted icing sugar until light and creamy. Add the flavourings, beat for 2 minutes or until the mixture is quite smooth and fluffy.

Cream Cheese Icing

This is a soft, thick, creamy topping. The creaminess of the cheese goes well with the tang of lemon or orange rind. Have the cheese at room temperature.

Beat cream cheese and icing sugar; add flavouring.

Lemon Cream Cheese Icing

100 g cream cheese
3/4 cup icing sugar
1–2 teaspoons finely grated lemon rind
2 teaspoons milk

Orange Cream Cheese Icing

100 g cream cheese
3/4 cup icing sugar
1–2 teaspoons finely grated orange rind
2 teaspoons milk

Honey Cream Cheese Icing

100 g cream cheese
3/4 cup icing sugar
1–2 teaspoons honey, warmed
2 teaspoons milk

Passionfruit Cream Cheese Icing

100 g cream cheese
3/4 cup icing sugar
1 tablespoon passionfruit pulp

Cream Cheese Icing method

Using electric beaters, beat cream cheese and sifted icing sugar together in small bowl until light and creamy. Add flavourings. Beat for 2 minutes or until the mixture is smooth and fluffy. Spread icing over cake, using a wide knife.

Fruit Glazes

Fruit glazes give a delicious, shiny finishing touch to cakes or fruit tarts. Simply warm apricot, strawberry or any other jam (or use fruit baby gel) with brandy, strain and brush over the cake.

Heat apricot jam and brandy together; strain.

Jam Glaze

1/4 cup jam
3 teaspoons brandy
Combine jam and brandy in small pan. Stir over low heat for 3 minutes or until jam has melted and mixture boils. Remove from heat and strain into a small bowl. Brush the warm jam mixture over the top of the warm cake.

Fruit Gel Glaze

110 g jar fruit baby gel
2 teaspoons brandy
Combine gel and brandy in small pan. Stir over low heat until gel has melted. Remove from heat. Brush warm mixture over cake.

Rich Chocolate Icing

60 g unsalted butter
100 g dark chocolate, chopped
1 tablespoon cream
Combine butter, chocolate and cream in small heatproof bowl. Stand over pan of simmering water, stir until butter and chocolate have melted and mixture is smooth. Cool slightly or until mixture is spreadable. Spread icing over cake using a wide knife.

Gently melt chocolate, butter and cream together.

Chocolate Sauce

100 g dark chocolate, chopped
1/3 cup cream
Combine chocolate and cream in small pan. Stir over low heat until chocolate has melted and mixture is smooth. Remove from heat, cool slightly, pour over cake.

Index